NORTH DAKOTA
impressions

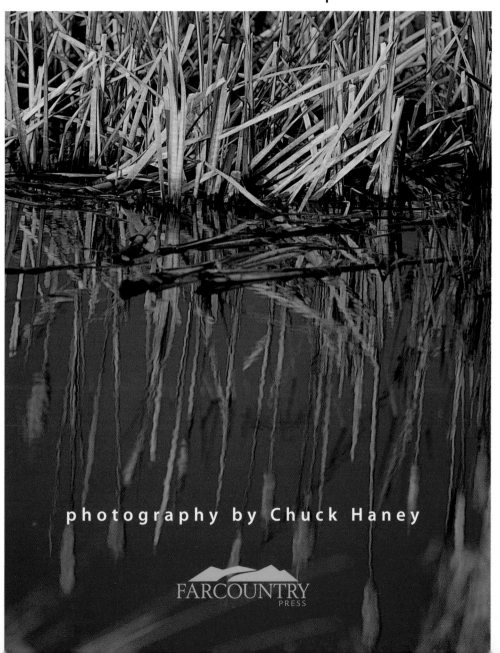

photography by Chuck Haney

FARCOUNTRY
PRESS

Right: Green ash trees are silhouetted against a sunrise at Sheyenne National Grasslands in Richland County.

Title page: Cattails reflected in a prairie pond at Sheyenne National Grasslands.

Front cover: Enjoying the view from cliffs above the Little Missouri River.

Back cover: At Bellfield a red scoria road leads to endless blue skies.

ISBN 10: 1-56037-259-1
ISBN 13: 978-1-56037-259-2

Photographs © 2003 by Chuck Haney
© 2003 by Farcountry Press

For more information on our books, write: Farcountry Press, P.O. Box 5630, Helena, MT 59604; call (800) 821-3874; or visit www.farcountrypress.com

Created, produced, and designed in the United States.
Printed in China.

17 16 15 14 13   3 4 5 6 7

Above: Wild horses graze in dusky light at Theodore Roosevelt National Park.

Facing page: Prairie wildflowers flourish in Ransom State Park, which is located along Sheyenne Valley National Scenic Byway.

A yellow-headed blackbird surveys
the landscape atop cattails in prairie
potholes at Lostwood.

Above: An aerial view of Fargo, 100,000-plus strong.

Facing page: The historic Fargo Theater has illuminated downtown since 1926.

The weathered face of an
eroded badlands formation at
Little Missouri National Grasslands
in McKenzie County.

Above: This unique 1943 barn in Dunseith also served as a dance hall.

Facing page: The proud relics of the 1883 DeMores Packing Plant in Medora. The town was founded by Marquis de Mores, who named the town after his wife and established the first large-scale meat-packing plant in North Dakota.

Above: Ideally suited for the prairie, coneflowers can tolerate dry soil and hot summer sun.

Right: Purple coneflowers line the shore of Lake Sakakawea, a favorite of Canada geese.

Above: Replica of Fort Mandan in winter. Lewis and Clark's Corps of Discovery constructed and wintered at Fort Mandan, near what is now Washburn, and named the encampment after their friendly neighbors, the Mandan, whose villages were a trade center for Northern Plains Indian tribes.

Facing page: A turret stands tall in defense of Fort Union, which was constructed in 1828 and served as the area's fur trade headquarters.

Following pages: Sunrise highlights ice formations on Lake Audubon near Garrison.

Above: Yellow pea flowers sprout from rocky outcroppings in Theodore Roosevelt National Park.

Facing page: Rivulets form and collect in pools after a rainfall in the badlands at Theodore Roosevelt National Park.

Above: Established by an act of the 1989 Legislative Assembly, Veterans Cemetery is located on a 35-acre tract of land in Fort Abraham Lincoln State Park south of Mandan.

Facing page: St. John's Church in Galchutt has drawn faithful parishioners since it was built in 1872.

23

Above: Wind sculpts snow to the contours of these badlands formations.

Facing page: Fresh snow blankets the grasslands near Wind Canyon in Theodore Roosevelt National Park, South Unit.

Above: Sunset over a prairie pothole in Lostwood National Wildlife Refuge.

Facing page: A freight train crosses the mighty Missouri River at Bismarck.

An almost unending field of immature sunflowers near Washburn. Sunflower seeds and oil are the third largest agricultural exports of North Dakota.

A field near Bottineau goldens with the cheerful blooms of sunflowers.

Above: A bison weather vane at Fort Union Trading Post National Historic Site near Williston on the Montana/North Dakota border. Goods were brought to Fort Union to trade with the Assiniboine, Blackfeet, Cree, Crow, Hidatsa, and Ojibway tribes for fur and bison hides.

Facing page: Bison graze and take in the morning sun at Sully's Hill National Wildlife Refuge near Devil's Lake.

A small marsh in the Sheyenne River Valley near Fort Ransom.

A canoe slices through the Missouri River at Cross Ranch State Park.

Above: Sandstone patterns at Theodore Roosevelt National Park, South Unit.

Facing page: In 1804 Lewis and Clark and the Corps of Discovery wintered here along the Missouri River near what is now Washburn.

Above: A pair of blue-winged teals feeds in a prairie pothole in Lostwood National Wildlife Refuge. The birds' diet consists of shallowly submerged vegetation, seeds, and small aquatic life.

Left: The many prairie potholes scattered throughout the mixed grasslands of Lostwood National Wildlife Refuge serve as much-needed breeding habitat for several species of Great Plains birds.

Above: Operations of a soybean harvest near Enderlin at day's end.
Soybeans are North Dakota's second largest agricultural export.

Facing page: Morning light on a field of canola near Killdeer.
The state leads the nation in production of canola.

Above: The unembellished, Art Deco–style capitol in Bismarck.

Facing page: A precarious but scenic ride along the ridgeline
above the Little Missouri River near Medora.

Above: Sign on an old barn in Beach.

Left: Horseback-riding through sweet yellow clover at Knife River Ranch in appropriately named Golden Valley.

Right: Effigies used by Mandan Indians at On-a-Slant Village to lure buffalo. Deserted by the end of the eighteenth century due to the devastating smallpox epidemic, On-a-Slant Village was one of nearly a dozen fortified cities of the Mandan Nation in the area.

Facing page: Inside a Mandan earthlodge at Knife River Indian Villages National Historic Site in Stanton. These wood-frame homes were covered with thick layers of earth, which kept temperatures cool in summer and warm in winter.

Above: A red admiral butterfly alights on marsh marigolds at Mirror Pool Wildlife Management Area, Sheyenne National Grasslands.

Left: Marsh marigolds in bloom at Mirror Pool Wildlife Management Area, Sheyenne National Grasslands. This spring plant favors wet meadows, marshes, and locations along moving water.

Above: The historic Fairview Lift Bridge crosses the frozen Yellowstone River.

Facing page: Feathery hoarfrost forms on a barbed-wire fence near Fryburg.

Above: A cold winter morning in a McKenzie County sugar-beet field.

Left: A rancher near Ross delivers feed to his cattle on a -20° morning.

Far left: Straw bales in dawn light on a frosty morning near Cartwright.

Left: Sunrise at historic Fort Union Trading Post National Historic Site.

Below: Pink tufts of prairie smoke seem to waft from their stems.

The Scandinavian Heritage Center is popular with visitors to Minot. A 230-year-old house was shipped in pieces from Sigdal, Norway, and reassembled at the center.

This Maltese Cross Cabin was Theodore Roosevelt's first home in the badlands.

Above: Evening light glows on a sandstone formation at Theodore Roosevelt National Park, South Unit.

Facing page: A quiet moment in a marsh at Turtle River State Park near Arvilla.

Storm clouds shape a dramatic
sunset at Williston.

Above: A classic red barn and grain bins near Williston are lit by sunrise.

Right: An oncoming storm creates a moody light over a field of wheat near Williston. Wheat is North Dakota's top agricultural export.

Above: A life-size cardboard cut-out of the late Lawrence Welk stands in the renovated main house of the farmstead that was his boyhood home in Strasburg.

Left: Cheery, pink blossoms outside the Grand Forks County Courthouse, which is listed on the National Register of Historic Places.

The proud countenance of a dramatic badlands
formation in the Little Missouri National Grasslands.

Right: A hillside overlooking the Pembina River at Walhalla wears the subtle hues of fall.

Below: Shining sumac leaves display their autumn tones at Turtle River State Park near Honeyford.

Above: A full moon sets at dawn in McKenzie County.

Facing page: In Rugby, the geographical center of North America, the 88-foot Northern Lights Monument reaches skyward from the prairie to recreate the spectacular Aurora Borealis.

Above: One of the tallest bridges in the country, the 1908 Hi-Line Railroad bridge crosses the Sheyenne River at Valley City.

Facing page: Historic Rainbow Arch Bridge stretches over the placid Sheyenne River.

Left: Red River of the North winds through the rural countryside between Fargo and Grand Forks.

Below: Paddling at sunset, Lake Metigoshe State Park.

Above: A prairie dog peers out from the safety of its burrow at the Cedar River National Grassland.

Right: These unusual formations, called cannonball concretions, are formed when a solid mineral mass is embedded in a mineral of another composition. The outer material then erodes, leaving the spherical core.

Dedicated in 1932, the International Peace Gardens on the North Dakota/Manitoba border serve as a monument to the peace between the United States and Canada.

Foxtail barley casts sparkles of light as the sun rises
over islands at Lake Sakakawea State Park.

Chuck Haney, a freelance photographer and writer, travels across the country in pursuit of scenic grandeur and interesting subjects. His landscape, agriculture, and outdoor sports photographs and articles have been published in numerous national and regional publications. More of his North Dakota images were published in *North Dakota Simply Beautiful* in 2001. He wrote and photographed *Badlands of the High Plains*, published in 2001, and contributed half the images in *Montana Wild and Beautiful* and *Glacier Wild and Beautiful*, published in 2000.